Ukraine Poems

David Jaffin

Ukraine Poems

February 9, 2022–
February 24, 2022

First published in the United Kingdom in 2022 by
Shearsman Books
50 Westons Hill Drive
Emersons Green
Bristol BS16 7DF

Shearsman Books Ltd Registered Office
30–31 St. James Place, Mangotsfield, Bristol BS16 9JB
(this address not for correspondence)

www.shearsman.com

ISBN 978-1-84861-872-5

Distributed for Shearsman Books in the U. S. A.
by Small Press Distribution, 1341 Seventh Avenue, Berkeley, CA 94710
E-Mail orders@spdbooks.org
www.spdbooks.org

Production, composition, & cover design: Edition Wortschatz,
a service of Neufeld Verlag, Cuxhaven/Germany
E-Mail info@edition-wortschatz.de, www.edition-wortschatz.de

Title painting:
Oil on canvas, without title 2021
Alfons Röllinger
Atelier Ruschweiler – Germany

Printed in Germany

Contents

With continuing thanks for
Marina Moisel
preparing
this manuscript

and to Alfons Röllinger
for his well-placed
painting

If I had to classify my poetry, it could best be done through the classical known "saying the most by using the least". The aim is thereby set: transparency, clarity, word-purity. Every word must carry its weight in the line and the ultimate aim is a unity of sound, sense, image and idea. Poetry, more than any other art, should seek for a unity of the senses, as the French Symbolists, the first poetic modernists, realized through the interchangeability of the senses: "I could hear the colors of her dress." One doesn't hear colors, but nevertheless there is a sensual truth in such an expression.

Essential is "saying the most by using the least". Compression is of the essence. And here are some of my most personal means of doing so turning verbs into nouns and the reverse, even within a double-context "Why do the leaves her so ungenerously behind". Breaking words into two or even three parts to enable both compression and the continuing flow of meaning. Those words must be placed back together again, thereby revealing their inner structure-atom-ising.

One of my critics rightly said: "Jaffin's poetry is everywhere from one seemingly unrelated poem to the next." Why? Firstly because of my education and interests trained at New York University as a cultural and intellectual historian. My doctoral dissertation on historiography emphasizes the necessary historical continuity. Today we often judge the past with the mind and mood of the present, totally contrary to their own historical context. I don't deny the past-romanticism and classical but integrate them within a singular modern context of word-usage and sensibility. Musically that would place me within the "classical-romantic tradition" of Haydn, Mozart, Mendelssohn, Brahms and Nielsen but at the very modern end of that tradition.

My life historically is certainly exceptional. My father was a prominent New York Jewish lawyer. The law never interested me, but history always did. A career as a cultural-intellectual historian was mine-for-the-asking, but I rejected historical relativism. That led me to a marriage with a devout German lady – so I took to a calling of Jesus-the-Jew in post-Auschwitz Germany. For ca. two decades I wrote and lectured all over Germany on Jesus the Jew. Thereby my knowledge and understanding of both interlocked religions became an essential part of my being. History, faith and religion two sides of me but also art, classical music and literature were of essential meaning – so many poems on poetry, classical music and painting.

Then Rosemarie and I have been very happily married for 61 years now. Impossible that a German and Jew could be so happily married so shortly after the war? I've written love poems for her, hundreds and hundreds over those 61 years, not only the love poems, as most are, of the first and often unfulfilling passion, but "love and marriage go together like a horse and carriage". Perhaps too prosaic for many poets?

When did I become a poet? My sister Lois wrote reasonably good poetry as an adolescent. I, only interested in sports until my Bar Mitzvah, a tournament tennis and table-tennis player, coached baseball and basketball teams, also soccer.

My sister asked whether I'd ever read Dostoyevsky. I'd only read John R. Tunis sports books and the sports section of the *New York Times* so I answered "in which sports was he active?" She said, rather condescendingly, "If you haven't read Dostoyevsky, you haven't lived." So I went to the library for the very first time and asked for a book by this Dostoyevsky. I received *Poor People*, his first book, that made him world famous. My mother shocked to see me reading and most especially a book about poor people said, "David, don't read that it will make you sad, unhappy – we, living in Scarsdale, weren't after all, poor people. From there it went quickly to my Tolstoy, Hardy and so on. In music it started with the hit parade, then *Lost in the Stars*, then the popular classics and with 15 or 16 my Haydn, Mozart, Schütz, Victoria ... And then at Ann Arbor and NYU to my artists, most especially Giovanni Bellini, Van der Weyden, Georges de la Tour, Corot and Gauguin ...

But it was Wallace Stevens' reading in the early 50s in the YMHA that set me off – he didn't read very well, but his 13 Ways of Looking at a Blackbird, Idea of Order at Key West, Two Letters (in *Poems Posthumous*), Peter Quince at the Clavier, The Snowman ... and the excellent obituary in *Time m*agazine plus the letter he answered some of my poems with compliments but "you must be your own hardest critic". That pre-determined my extremely self-critical way with a poem. Please don't believe that prolific means sloppy, for I'm extremely meticulous with each and every poem.

My poems were published in the order written and I'm way ahead of any counting ... The poem is a dialogical process as everything in life. The words come to me not from me, and if they strike or possibly join-a-union then I become desparate, read long-winded poets like Paz to set me off – he's very good at odd times. Those poems need my critical mood-mind as much as I need their very specially chosen words – not the "magic words" of the romantics, but the cleansed words of Jaffin – Racine used only 500 words. My words too are a specially limited society, often used, but in newly-felt contexts.

O something very special: I have a terrible poetic memory. If I had a good one as presumably most poets, I'd write say one poem about a butterfly, and every time I see/saw a butterfly it would be that one, that poem. But I forget my poems, so each butterfly, lizard, squirrel ... is other-placed, other-mooded, other-worded, other-Jaffined. That's the main reason why I am most certainly the most prolific of all poets.

Shakespeare is the greatest of us: his sonnets live most from the fluency and density of his language. I advise all future poets to keep away from his influence and the poetic greatness of The Bible.

Yours truly
David Jaffin

P. S.: As a preacher the truth (Christ) should become straight-lined, timelessly so, but as a poet it's quite different. What interests me most are those contradictions which live deeply within all of us, not only in theory, but daily in the practice. And then the romantics have led me to those off-sided thoroughly poetic truths that mysteriously not knowing where that darkened path will lead us.

If only

darkness
is to be

seen is it
looking

through
the invis

ible depth
of your self-

reclaiming-
past.

Dream

as Word de
termines not

only its own
means of

expressing
an exclusive
ly irredeem

able–past.

Time-telling *(5)*

a) pictures An art

ist's time–tell

ing picture
s signifying

b) his most-per

sonal–raison–

d'être To his
right his role–

model Haydn
pen and paper

c) at hand and

a recognition

plague of Is
rael's 40

year life–

d) span Closer at

hand Jesus'

penetrat
ing all-

assuming-pre
sence On the

e) window

sill my Rose
marie at

various
time and

place-expos
ure

s.

A single

immovably-
visible-star

at this
early morn

ing light-
phase witness

ing the poet'
s word-deter

mining-re
solve.

Our house (3)

> *a) and garden*
>
> vintage 1937–
>
> 38 the same
> as Rosemarie
>
> and myself
>
>
> *b) One of the*
>
> oldest in
> this modern
>
> post–war
> suburban
>
> town despite
>
>
> *c) all it re*
>
> mained her
> private time-
>
> elusive most
> indwelling-re
>
> sort.

"You call the (3)

a) shots" confid

ing words

from the golf
er to his

b) caddy to

choose the best

wood or iron
But also more

household You
Rosemarie shall

c) decide the

day's course

But that "shot"
has something

ominous about
it.

Exampled *(3)*

a) No one

knows (not e
ven the so–

called expert

b) s) which way

Corona will
mutate next

She's become
the best

c) example

for what

we call
personal-freed

om.

Good starter (5)

a) s especially

with T. S.

Eliot may re
main memor

able while

b) not even

"love at
first sight"

insures a fu
ture-happi

ness. A

c) bright

late winter
day may e

ven lift the
usual sun

d) beyond its

lowly-expect

ant-path
but bright

e) hopes often

remain with

out a suffi
ciently-secure

ground-base.

If one has *(3)*

a) acquired in

time "a

mind for win
ter" will

b) only loosen

its half–per

manent–hold
with those

seldom spring

c) thoughts as

with the ap
pearance

of the first
innocent

snow–drop
s.

No-lady *(3)*

a) For her no

remains the

first ungen
uine respon

b) se only then

does she be

gin to real
ise the why

and where
fore of a

c) tentative

ly–assumed

if–rarely–
expressive–

agreement.

Hay pigs *(3)*

a) Their adver

tisement for
"hay pigs"

Just the
freedom you'

b) ve always

wanted for

rolling-free
But not to

be forgot
en what or

c) who has enjoy

ed such a

self-satisfy
ing life taste

s better as
well.

It's diffi (3)

 a) cult not to

 love a woman

 as attract
 ive and fine

 b) ly-sensitive

 as my Rose

 marie but it
 becomes less

 difficult
 when her mood

 c) s fully embrace

 such indwell
 ing loveli

 ness.

Such a (2)

a) fully encom

passing Feb

ruary after
noon bright

tens Rose

b) marie's smile

to mid-
summer Ital

ianate swim-
time pleasur

ings.

New-type (3)

a) woman A work-

type woman

You can see
it from the

b) manly cloth

es and the

inadequate
smile that

c) seems to

say I'm the

financial–
serious new–

type woman.

A-time-for- (2)

a) rest We all

need–a–time–

for–rest trans
lating I've had

enough for the
day body and

b) soul lacking

their indigen

ous desire for
a spacious

self-accept
ance.

Word ripe (2)

a) Those spec

ial-unexpect
ed-times

when the
poems don't

require extra
time for

b) dress rehear

sals They're

ready and set
come-what-

may word-
ripe.

In these *(3)*

a) specially

brighten

ed times of
late winter

b) when shadow

s neverthe

less seem
especially

cold–forsak

c) en as a woman

so–voiced
complete

ly–out–of
place–

ground–based.

When I stopp (4)

a) *ed preaching*

(at least for
public use)

b) *and began*

poetising
the Pietists

felt I'd be
gun stepping

c) *down from*

Jacob's ladd

er No I al
ways felt my

d) *self (preach*

ing or poetis

ing aside) as
Luther fully

ground-based.

G. M. J *(in memoriam)* *(7)*

a) Always-on-

time's rhythm
for daily

b) work a partner

ship as the

one with God
himself money

and good-work-
wise He called

c) it "Make mon

ey do good

(and that
extra divid

end) "having

d) fun" Though

he'd fully
prepared for

the funeral
came at the

e) wrong time

Christmas

vacation
many failed

to show-up

f) (even some

very import
ant ones

money-wise)
he died as

g) everyone

else to death'

s self-invok
ing-rhythm

not-his-own.

Mapping-life *(6)*

a) out He'd learn

ed from his

very–success
ful–father

b) the virtues

of free will

His life was
his-for-the-

asking yet

c) strangely e

nough however
much he

sought for the
right wife –

d) those dozens

of blind date

s She appear
ed in a for

eign yes alien

e) land for a

life's route

of over 60
years happy-to

getherness
And with her

f) the totally un

expected call

ing to serve
INRI Christ

the Jew.

6:45 *(5)*

a) lights on

across–the–

way though
still in re

b) ceptive-dark

ness Light

does deter
mine life

but this one

c) artificial

ly–secure
for a gen

uine (if
old–fashion
ed)

d) family

of 4 husband

wife and 2
young child

e) ren not the

becoming popu

lar two wo
men and a

dog.

On-the-road (4)

a) He's on-the-

road now

(don't expect
too much

b) David or

you'll be

let-down)
that long 4

hour drive
My life's

c) trip remain

ed at time

s a space–
accomodat

ing voyage
through per

d) haps pre-de

termining

but neverthe
less unknown–

terrain.

My life's (3)

a) voyage as my

mother's al

ways 22 Oak
Lane 22 in

b) Malmsheim

now our 13

and 9 resid
ences Why 22

Perhaps be
cause of my

c) central theo

logical break-

through Psalm
22 as The First

fully-sourced-
Gospel.

Out-lined *(3)*

a) Just this

early morn

ing out-line
of houses

b) still most

ly darkly-

dreamed-as
leep Is that

the biblical
way as well

c) an ever-clear

er out-line

of The Good
Lord's time

ly-messag
ing.

The way and wherefore *(5)*

a) Has my life

been routed
as my eldest

b) sister Doris

through

these mostly
read–through

book–shelved–

c) inhabitant

s or my teach
er's pre–dat

ing my future–
course Neither

d) one nor the

other but an

invisible
hand guiding

me step by
apparent

e) ly errant

step to the

me of my
now indwell

ing–self.

"The handwrit (3)

a) ing's on the

wall" When the

High Court in
Germany allowed

b) a "terrorist"

anti–Israel anti–

semitic group
freedom of

speech here
The "handwriting'

c) s on the wall"

Hitler has won

they'll soon
be a "Jew–

free" Germany.

Dead leave *(3)*

a) s but a

mirrored re

flection
of–what–once

b) had-been

So will it

appear at
your grave'

c) s name-sake

stoned–in

apparent–
remem

brance.

Spoiled *(3)*

a) children

rarely live–

up to their
parent's

b) name-sake

And I the

only son in
a Jewish fam

ily the young
est as well

c) and until a

dolescence

as my mother
exclaimed

"mostly an
gelic".

Something (3)

a) remained miss

ing in that

old Polish
town It wasn'

b) t anything

the young

sters could
feel those rhy

thmic foot
steps once

c) so familiar

but now only

echoing
their century-

old-Jewish-
past.

Only 3% sur (3)

a) vived those Ger

man death–

camps so–
efficient

b) ly organi

sed even

zoo–animal
s were treat

c) ed with the

necessary

untouch
able–re

spect.

A Woman (4)

a) self display

ing body-

wise dance-
wise her

b) unreconcil

able past

grandfath
ering a min

or–Nazi–death

c) camp sexual

ly misused
as a child

On display
as if such

d) catharsis

could lessen

a pene
trating past–

performan
ce.

For Lukas (4)

a) *In an increa*

singly secu

larised–post–
Christian

b) *society our*

fundament

al–Christ
ian faith

shouldn't be

c) *denied but*

should never
theless (in

its own parti
cular way)

d) *remain self-*

deceptive

ly conceal
ed?

One call *(3)*

a) ed it "a dis

play piece"

pedestal
ly to a

b) height of

self-import

ance or was
it that wo

c) man bodied

to a rhythm

ic past-time
self-appre

ciation.

This early

morning dark
ness has ta

ken-on a
sense of con

tinuing (if
at times)

impenetra
ble) dialog

ue.

Origin (3)

a) Does spring

actually be
gin with a

tensing-sen

b) se-of-expec

tation or
with the in

itial ground-

c) touch of a

fragile yell
ow and white

colored-flo
wering.

Holocaust-curse *(4)*

a) Now that

the German
high court

has allowed
an anti-Is

b) rael (anti-

semitic) free

dom of speech
after Merkel

allowed an
uncontroll

c) ed influx of

our Moslem

enemies 2015
I sense the

end of Jew
ishness here

d) and a perpet

uation of

the last
ing Holocau

st–curse.

As there *(4)*

a) remain so few

truly devout

Christian
s poetry–

b) minded and

a few more

secularis
ed poetry-lo

vers–open
to even a

c) small dose

of Christ

ianed–verse
The poet re

mains as Du

d) Fu caught in

that similar
tangle of his

Confucian–
Taoist–anti

thesis.

A prelude (2)

a) These rain

s seem to
be thinning–

out somewhat
finely sourc

b) ed as if

spring was

in the air
if as yet

scarcely ground–
based.

Call them (3)

a) Nazis They

may have been

our fathers
grandfather

b) s... Please

call them

Nazis not Ger
mans they're

c) different

we've learned

better
Call them

Nazis.

Poetry and (3)

a) money have

never real

ly rhymed–to
gether The one

b) may be beauty

conscious

though more
often than

not a penny–
a-line The

c) other a true

measure of

one's self-in
habiting i

deas-of-gran
deur.

Heavily o *(3)*

a) vercast

they call
ed it as

if such
darkening

b) clouds had

been heavily-

weighted
or perhap

s because
they're

c) weighing

heavily on

your time-
suspending

thought
s.

Package- *(5)*

a) deals Poetry

or any other

art's not
necessar

b) ily a pack

age–deal of

all–or–noth
ing I unpack

aged my love

c) ly wife day

by day year
by year and

discover
ed many un

d) suspecting-

treasure

s but also
certain thing

e) s that did

n't–seem–to–

rhyme–so–
well–togeth

er.

As poetry (4)

a) *and wine seem*

to cultivate

each other
as in much

b) *high-level*

Persian and

Chinese verse
I still pre

fer the in

c) *ebriating*

quality of
open-spaced

distancing
s and of the

d) *intimacy of*

touched-re

fined femin
ine-sensibil

ities.

False (3)

a) news remain

s what you'

re unwill
ing to hear

b) But why

read it any

way if it'
s simply

c) timing the

other side

of your
self–inhab

iting cause.

Gerhard Rich *(4)*

a) ter at 90 no

interest until

now but his
love of C. D.

Frederich and

b) Hammershøi

much my view
That his paint

ings speak-on–
their-own

right so do

c) my poems

Those 2 paint
ings of the

candles and
that fine

late abstract

d) landscape

first rate I
must wait and

most especial
ly see more…

A respoken domain (3)

a) Rosemarie'
s fully-recept
ive kisses

b) speak more
of her soul-
length than

I'd ever real
ised before

Just the look

c) of her in
light blue a
wakens slumber

ing and more-
than-evident-

desiring
s.

Contrast (4)

a) *ing poetic-time-*

lengths Rose

marie modestly
posed in front

b) *of our once*

22 Oak Lane

red brick Georg
ian-styled

house person

c) *ed in its own*

right window
ing poetic-

lengths while
Rosemarie the

d) *always unseen*

source of

this continu
ing poetic-

flow.

The-hard- *(2)*

a) way Never com

pete in marr

iage (as she
learned the–

hard–way) be

b) cause good

marriage
s retain

their comple
mentary–unif

ying–claim
s.

Rooms too (3)

a) retain their

always change

able light-
qualities

b) very much the

way our mood

s (most effect
ively feminine

ly-sourced)

c) curtain invis

ible deeper–

retained-ex
pressive

ness.

Blues *(3)*

a) Is it Rose

marie's light
blue or that

landscaping

b) expressive

Bellini-blue

and that e
ver-change

able heaven
ly-blue that

c) denies what

ever blues may

pre-deter
mine my

daily-poet
ic-fare.

Hammershøi' *(3)*

a) s quietude

s those meta

physical
De Hooch's

b) open-space

s doesn't

domesti
cate them

c) but create

s an inti

mate if ab
stract-famil

iarity.

Do wake-up (3)

a) bells as

those French

ones for "Bro
ther John"

b) sound lin

guistical

ly other
wise than

say Ameri
can ones

c) for wake-

up call

ing an o
therwise

in-tuned
tonality?

"First come (6)

a) first served"

Our daily

3 or 4 fat-
appetizing–

b) walnuts

attract those

ugly over-
sized crows

mouth-fitt

c) ing-special

ity broken-
shells high-

dive while
our eucumeni

c) cal-squirrel

s Ulysses

and Samuel
usually too–

late-comers

e) with that

innocent yet
self-demand

ing look of

f) they were real

ly intended
only for our–

own-squirrel
ing-need

s.

Double-lensed (6)

a) Does this

windowed-
light help

sustain a

b) double-view

the one fram
ed-support

ive the other
keen-eyed

c) as a treed-

immensing
bird's Are

photograph

c) ing-eyes

as Hanni's

or Lukas'
also double–

lensed Does

e) photography

despite its
camera–supp

ortive need
s display an art

because the

f) eye's-special

ly–desired–in

sights remain
subjective

ly–sourced.

February *(3)*

a) 12 Uschi's

and Solvey'

s birthday
ing our most

personal two-

b) sided-respon

se Lincoln'

s as well
two-sided

North and
South and a

c) still vastly

divided na

tion he was
elected to

maintain
unified.

"Nothing's (3)

a) new under the

sun" although

we're still
discovering

untold ocean

b) ic-depths and

a spaceless-
universe where

as artists and
thinkers con

tinue to per

c) spective

new insight
s of the

perhaps al
ready-other

wise-known.

The touch (3)

> *a) of cold-steel*
>
> or of iced–
>
> branches
> insinuate
>
> s a depth
>
>
> *b) of long-un*
>
> recalled–
> sensation
>
> s or remem
>
>
> *c) bering*
>
> that existen
> cial emptied–
>
> down roller-
> coaster-feel
>
> ing as a teen
> ager at Rye'
>
> s Playland.

We can't *(3)*

a) relive the

past only in

dreams but
then other

b) wise exper

ienced But

that past
keeps reliv

c) ing us with

out our real

ising its–pur
posing–intent

ions.

Movies re (3)

a) *tain an atmos*

pheric–dimen

sion poetical
ly–express

b) *ive which*

remains large

ly outside
the scope of

theater's
raison d'ê

c) *tre Is that*

perhaps why

movies move
us multi–di

mension
ally.

When the

last(ing)
snow melt

s as dream
s in to a

long-forgot
ten memory-

span.

Photos (3)

a) may be seen

as but-a-

momentary-
expressive

b) ness but

the more of

ten we-scan
through-

their-evoca
tive-presen

c) ce the more

they become

timeless
ly-conceiv

ed.

Aschbacher (7)

a) Berg Hotel

For over 60

years it's be
come a part

b) of our very

festive-be

ing with that
panoramic

hill-top

c) view of the

Bavarian Alp

s Birthday
s (the spec

ial ones) and

d) anniversar

ies celebrat
ed here That

winding up-
staired-road

e) now straight

ened-out mess

aging perhap
s its own

self-encom

f) passing sea

sonal iden
tity We've

aged with
this ho

f) tel and per

haps it feels
(despite those

renovation
s) aging-with-

us-as-well.

Re-establish (5)

a) ing My almost

105 year–old–
mother learn

ed in time

b) (specially

after her hus
band's tragic

fall) to re
establish

c) herself with

the times

and person
s Although

estranged

d) from a world

that became
ever–more

hardly legi
ble she dott

ed its i's

e) and crossed

its t's with
her own per

sonal other
wise–identi

ty.

Two route (3)

a) s They learn

ed in short–

time that one
can't talk–

b) out-diplomat

ically a war

that's long
been planned

step–by–step
for Russia'

c) s (Putin's)

reestablish

ing his–most–
personal

ised Soviet
Union.

On an awaken (3)

a) ing mid-Febru

ary Sunday

morning these
long apparent

b) ly-dead-win

tered-tree

s seem to
be growing

earth and

c) time-wise in

to their pre
vious stately-

leafed-stat
ure.

Dancing *(4)* *(for Neil)*

a) as a sport

of most any
kind seem

b) s to free

the body of
its most lim

iting self–
inhabiting

c) homestead

It's a kind

of self–dia
logue while re

leasing its

d) consuming de

sire for a
rhythmic ex

pressive
ness.

Shakespeare

as a poet
master of

the word'
s fluent

time-flow
and the den

sity of its
pre-sourced

finality.

"Just loosen-

up" she said
as a subtle

means of
more than an

internal
yes export

able self-
expressive

ness.

Time sharing

s He sought

to discover
the initial

intent of
life's impul

sings if e
lusively time-

sharing
s.

Otherwise (2)

a) One only

becomes a
genuine poet

when its lan
guage enable

b) s you to

realise

things word-
like apparent

ly-other
wise.

Unqualified (3)

a) What if at
the Beijing
Olympics
you don't

b) qualify for
your self-in
tended disci
pline That's
a question
plaguing

c) many even un
athletic
self-desir
ing young
sters.

The devil's advocate (2)

a) as S. L. most

always taking–

the–other
side of the

argument may
lead to a

b) self-reveal

ing dialogue

despite the
possible under

lying–side–
effect

s.

High-horsed (3)

a) For the multi-

talented (more-
explicitly-

multi-know

b) ledgeable)

discover
ing a part

ner equally-
accomplish

ed may become

c) desirable to

step-down a
bit from one's

high-horsed
posture.

Swiss-Ger (4)

a) man's without

a grammar

Write it
your way

b) spell it

your way as

Shakespeare
did It doesn'

t-much-matter
Dialects the-

c) true-linguist

ic-initiat

ors grammar
less Why con

form to an
artificial

d) grammar when

language in

itiates it
self at-such-

a-ground-base.

Interluding (3)

a) When this

little black
bird landed

so unobtru
sively on my

b) balcony what

became of his

very wordless
perhaps even

thought

c) less just-sit

ting-there
interlud

ing between
landing-right

s?

Identity- *(3)*

a) cause for

most German

s a church
less Christ

b) ianless

bright mid–

February
Sunday morn

ing day-off
Not more-or–

c) less-than-

that from a

once tradit
ional–identi

ty-cause.

Interim (3)

a) phase We may

have been

created with
a need for

faith in a

b) God creating

and guid
ing His world

now travel
ing its own

c) peaceless

self-destruct

ive perhaps
s interim–

phase?

On-and-off *(4)*

a) Should I say

it or conceal

it from the o

b) thers The one

say you're a

poet with that
Keatsian

beauty-truth

c) calling the

others say we'
re not requir

ed to say or

d) write what

may become
personally

hurting on–
and-off.

Pre-determin (3)

a) ed My balcony'

s hard–wooden-
surfacing

keeps pre–de

b) termining

the abstract
length of

what could
have been a

more person

c) al intimate

still life
kind–of–ex

pressive
ness.

Is it the (4)

a) translat

ions or are

so many of
these very

b) early Chinese

poems more

like a faith
ful listing

of what's

c) poetically

conceived
Really good

poetry should
imply contin

d) uing-varied-

levels-of–

thought-ex
tending-mean

ing.

Some poem (4)

a) *s I reread*

through

the particu
lar focus of

b) *friends and*

intimate read

ers All my
poems are read

that way to

c) *Rosemarie*

on a daily
most personal

here-and-no(w)
wheres-else

If I had mar

d) *ried another*

woman would
those poem

s have be
come differ

ent as
well.

American *(3)*

a) *squirrel*

s fat and
grey failed

to squirrel

b) *me Ours here*

small and
lithe-brown

in their

c) *highly-spac*

ed-locating
design's

squirrel
ling.

These late (3)

a) winter day

s increas

ingly long
er even their

b) twilight

seems to be

holding a
timeless-

spell as if

c) magically

aware of the
spring's ground–

based–color
ings.

Dream (5)

a) Can one real

ise dream

as the-o
ther–side–of–

b) self what-

could–have–

been pre–
determining

its own self–

c) imagining

s Or is dream

often a mis
print of what

actually

d) happened Is

dream a re
minder of

beware-of–

e) future-dang

ers don't
ever again

play-with–
fire.

Self-decept *(4)*

a) ion Out at

sea alone

with one's
own time-ex

b) tending

thought

s The sea
calmed to

those still
attuned to

c) tentative

ly-aware
d-phrasing

s that might
as well im

d) *ply a spec*

ial kind of

necess
ary-self-de

ception.

He didn't (3)

a) *fully under*

stand that

poem may
have actual

b) *ly under*

stood his

self-con
cealing way

of denying

c) *what remain*

ed outside
his scientific-

analytic-
scope.

Eye-sense (2)

a) *may poise*

unanswer

ed question
ing its own

raison d'ê

b) *tre or e*

ven the lack
of a self–

certain
ing–respon

se.

Actions (2)

> *a) may actually*
>
> "speak loud
>
> er than word
> s" that keep
>
> resounding

> *b) through*
>
> your fully
> activated
>
> timely–ap
> peal
>
> s?

Fired- (2)

> *a) up Those*
>
> children
> as Aron
>
> who once
> "played–

b) with-fire"

may once a

gain become
fired–up

with flam
ing-desire

s.

Misconcept (2)

a) ions One of

those recurr
ing miscon

ception
s that o

b) thers react

in–much–the–

same–way
as your

thought–in
tention

s.

Has "know (2)

a) ing-what-you

want" become

a kind of
half-way–

there as
those pri

b) mitive hunt

ers' wall–

painting
s of a fin

alising-
taste.

Turning-the- *(3)*

a) pages-back

While turn

ing-the-page
s-back through

b) his life-

view became

so alive
once again

c) reactivat

ing his

let's-try-
that-once-a

gain.

"Twice-told *(6)*

a) tales" Was Miss

Blackburn'
s cleaning–

off her 2nd

b) grade black

board a
means of say

to herself
and her young

c) pupils (your)

life too may re

main full of
2nd-time-nec

essary-start

d) ers Sweet

things as a
fully-sourc

ed-kiss or
an After

e) Eight choco

late-timing

fine but
what's over-

f) sweet dis

tracts from its

pre-posit
ive-intent

ions.

A tasty-ap (3)

a) peal That pretty

waitress
s' sugar–

sweet-look

b) made me quite

aware of
those straw

berry tarts

c) she'd soon

be serving–
up for more

than just a
tasty–appeal.

Word-sending (3)

a) s Such slight

early–morning
puffy clouds

somehow remind

b) ing of young

school child
ren constantly

aware of their
teacher'

s time–re

c) sounding

though suffi
ciently-ap

parent–word–
sending

s.

Closed-door *(7)*

a) s For most

children
their parent

al closed–

b) doors seem

to inhabit
something

most especial
ly-unknown

yet awaken

c) ing various

kinds and spe
cies of self–

imagin
ings where

as the closed

d) doors of the

very sick
and dying

as with
Uncle Morton

our Esauian

e) dentist a-

hairy–hunter
oft–athleti

cally–unleash
ed and Grand

f) pa Jaffin'

s every

second–
year's dy

ing–phase

g) left us with

the awe of
an unknown

phantom
ed–being.

Chinese (4)

a) Why were

those often-
exiled-poet

s whose crit
icism of

b) the emperor

left them at

distance
s from house

and home hard

c) ly-ever (or

so it seem
s) allowed to

bring wife
and children

d) along result

ing as well

in some-very-
fine-longing

ful-poetry.

Dead-end *(3)*

a) ed "I told you

so"'s display
ing an I-know-

better-than-
you-attitude

b) competitive-

comparat

ive sense-
of-super

iority That
one-way-street'

c) s bound to

lead to a

much-deser
ved dead-

end.

Ukraine (4)

a) They asked

for the most
necessary

heavy weapon
s the German

b) s responded

with a moral

support that
may have lift

ed their own
past–time–mili

c) tary–guilty–

conscience

to the height
of an empty–

handed moral–
superior

d) ity and for

a bonus ("extra

dividend") an
apparently

lost–cause.

Putin's extra *(4)*

a) dividend On

Valentine'

s Day you
could feel

spring in
the air and

b) the spread

ing delicate

ly-colored-
snow-drops

and crocus
yellow and

white and

c) the pleasing

faces of young
and not-so-

young-lover
s but hard

as you may
listen not yet

d) the blood-red

sounds of Pu

tin's expan
sive–annex

ation Ukrain
ian war.

Resumé (3)

a) A. J. P. Taylor

an Oxford his
torian once

preached
(quite differ

b) ently from

the so-call

ed enlighten
ed–historian

s) that we
learn from

c) past mistake

s to make

just-the-op
posite-one

s for fu
ture's sake.

Life reviv (4)

a) *ing-instin*

cts By mid–Febru

ary the dark
ness has less

ened its

b) *grasp on our*

daily consc
iousness of

spring's
first ground–

based fragile

c) *flower's ex*

pressive–ur
gings Valen

tine's Day

d) *well-placed*

for our own
life–reviv

ing instin
cts.

Taizé

Repetition

's a usual
liturgi

cal means
for a self–

attunement
with the

biblical word
As dance it

releases our
self–inhibit

ing–homestead
steadily in

creasing
the–rhythmic–

designs–of
word–conscious

ness But that
repetitive–

sameness
can also dull

our mind
from its

deepening–
creative–

awareness.

Routine *(3)*

a) of most any

kind become

s in time
a safety

b) protect

ive mean

s for deny
ing the un

expected

c) upsetting

the satis
faction of

the-always-
familiar.

That "I (4)

a) feel at home

here" a com

pliment for
those who

b) have satis

fied his self–

securing–
needs I per

sonally only

c) "feel at

home" with
Rosemarie

usually seat

d) ed right-a

cross-the-way
from my ad

miring-toge
therness.

Forbidden- *(4)*

a) fruit That for

bidden–fruit

whether a
special brand

b) of apples or

whatever

partakes as the
Snake itself

of change
able–tempta

c) tions of

power–sexual

ity or even
the Beethov

ian Prometh
ian inspira

d) tional-source

remains Now

as alway
s The Good

Lord Himself!

Self-expressive (3)

a) ness Dog-owner

s of what
ever breed

usually
feel spec

b) ial pleas

ure in releas

ing their
domesticat

ed "best

c) friend" for

the open
fields of

self–express
iveness.

The eye- *(2)*

a) length of a

Chinese diag

onal paint
er transform

ing space in

b) to the most

effective guar
antee of in

explicit
time-tell

ing
s.

Is the emp *(3)*

a) ty canvas of

that dialogi

cal Chinese paint
er the empty pa

b) per-pad of

the poet's

calling to
that distinct

c) ive-impress

ing-of here

and–now–and–
nowhere-

else.

Brought (3)

a) *back to mind*

after 65

years that
initial path

b) *of Faulkner'*

s As I Lay Dy

ing its dis
tances and

still resound

c) *ing echoing*

s as if I
had become so

untimely-descri
bed.

Dad *(4)*

a) That feel

ing for those
spacious

ly-unresolved–

b) moments and

the so-dis
tinctive–

instinct
ual-sound

c) s of another'

s footstep

s fading-out
beyond the

d) tradition

al realms of

one's own
here-and–

now.

Señora Lopez *(3)*

a) our sensitive

Spanish teach

er described
an unknown

b) cousin for

some 30-odd-

years who'd
experienced

much the same
things as

c) she herself

as if shadow

ing-her-un
timely-wherea

bout
s.

Maker and (4)

a) *measure Man*

the maker

and measure
of all-thing

b) *s neverthe*

less in need

of the necess
ary rain and

sun for life'

c) *s time-growth*

s and of
love the es

d) *sential in*

gredient
for a truly

meaningful
time-span.

They claim (4)

a) ed Jerry the

faithful

guardian of
house and

b) home unable

to assume

life's daily
nitty-grit

ty chore

c) s must have

experien
ced repetit

ive dream
s of fear

d) ful time-ex

tending

empty-hand
ed loneli

ness.

Question (5)

a) ing Lukas

Does your
pre-assum

ing camera

b) or your time

ly-inspir
ed-insight

s pre-deter
mine your

c) short-stor

ied life-im

pelling mov
ies or

should I

d) rather ask

myself wheth
er Poem hasn'

t pre-concei

e) ved my own

specially-
realised–

word–per
spective

s.

Neil's per (4)

a) haps the-only-

one-left to

re-confirm
my almost–

b) totally-

lost–child

hood–memor
ies and if

he should

c) die before

me would
they become

perhaps al
ternately–

d) sourced-

through un

expect
ed–dream–

flow
s.

Outsider (3)

a) s If we can'

t genuine

ly-timely
understand

b) ourselves How

can we ex

pect those
always–out

siders to

c) penetrate

such time
ly-encompass

ing-myster
ies.

The poet' (5)

a) s room dou

bly wooden–

sourced the
ceiling and

b) side-expos

ures of 1937–

38-vintage
whereas my

windowed

c) and door-

side view'
s almost–con

temporarily
dated Does

d) that help

explain my

here ten
sioned past

birth-time

c) Nazi-time

and now fully
self-reclaim

ing Rose
marie-time.

Corona- *(3)*

a) spite Can we

really spite

Corona's pre-
establish

ing-hold liv

b) ing freely

once again
as if noth

ing had real
ly occurr

ed except

c) the fearful

possibil
ity of a

nother dead
lier-mutat

ion.

Male-emanci (4)

a) pation? They're

fully aware
(however mod

est they ap

b) pear) of their

power over
us poor-un

emancipat
ed-males

they possess

c) us with a pret

ty face and
bodily-enti

cing-form
while now

they're pre

d) paring to

take-over
the-business-

place-as-
well.

Word-sense *(5)*

a) He awakened

with but a

single word
that seemed

b) foreign at

first too

(shall we
call it high-

brow) useable for

c) a "thirty day

s for a more
powerful

vocabulary"
that over–

d) view of cap

tured Captivat

ing's the
word it mean

s but past
that initial

e) sounding-out

it does cap
tivate in more

than just a
singular-

sense.

Workshop' (6)

a) s the name of

a fine English

poetry maga
zine year

b) s back then

poetry can

also imitate
a workshop

of words–ex

c) pressive

ly–useable
or (for that

matter) staid
ly–unaccept

d) able or over-

wrought with

too–much–a
dolescent–

enthusiasm

e) Its good edi

tor Norman Hid
den used red

for the appar
ently fully–

f) reliable and

black as my

own poems for
the hidden

up–in–coming.

"One thing (6)

a) at a time"

may seem diffi

cult even con
trary to those

b) multi-talent

ed uneased

with a contra
punctal time–

c) span and that

self-perpetua

ting need to
get-thing

s-done At
84 my mind

d) and feeling

s "off-to-

the-race-
track" while

it may take
much self-

e) persuasion

to arise

from a com
fortable

chair and
hasten my

f) feet from

their pre-estab

lishing ground-
based-ten

sure.

On the move (3)

a) his eyes

intending litt

le children'
s baby-eyed–

b) response the

freedom-e

voking fam
ily dog–

pull and last
(but certain

not least) the
appearance

c) of attract

ive-young–

ladie
s.

Symbolic *(3)*

a) act Pulling

these poetry

room's blue
curtains o

b) pen to the

time–extend

ding sun's a
substan

cial–symbol
ic–act for

c) resourc

ing–evid

ently–cer
tained–imag

ining
s.

He respond (3)

a) ed to Nielsen'

s symphonie

s with "they'
re not dark

b) like most

Scandina

vian folk
songs" yes

the bright

c) and reclaim

ing optimism
of the Danish

life–resilent–
aspiring

s.

His mind- *(3)*

a) sense became

haunted with a

new-daring
ly-express

b) ive-imagery

that he be

gan to quest
ion the limit

c) ations of Dr

Johnson's

self-commend
ing upright-

grammar.

Arabesque

Bushy long-
tailed squir

rels rhyme
these naked

ly-branch
ed-trees in

to something
like a French-
evolving-ara

besque.

Poetic-li (2)

a) cense Does

one call that

poetic-li
cense Per

sian quality

b) medieval

poets wine-
inhabiting

their Mus
lim freed

om-fare.

Alternat (5)

a) ing feeling

s Tiny flower

s dotting
the front

b) lawn with per

haps untimely

expectat
ions and that

tree right-a

c) cross-the-

way blossom
ing with e

ven further
hopeful-sign

d) s yet the

air's cold

and penetrat
ingly-winter

ed while I'
m hardly

e) blessed with

such inbetween

ed–alternat
ing–expectat

ions.

Phantoms *(2)*

a) Lurid city

lights depth
ed to the

fears of un
told danger

s Were they

b) only dreamed-

phantoms
of what re

mains of an
unreconcil

ing–past.

Feet-find *(4)*

a) for those

high-walker

s display
ing distant

b) expectat

ions their

rarely-felt
sense of

footstep'

c) s softly-re

sponding–car
pets More like

ly the faint–

d) barren-claim

s-of their
own feet–

find's-echo
ings.

Suburban New Yorkers (4)

a) *If I were*

a woman as
my two eld

b) *er sister*

s still old–

fashion
ed marriage-

oriented I

c) *would most*

fear losing
my time-re

calling look
s and my

d) *husband's*

daily work

in that
"city-of-(all)-

sins".

When music (4)

a) *becomes most*

poetic in

those early
romantic

b) *composer'*

s almost

saddenly
sense-of–

loss as

c) *those exil*

ed Chinese
poets long

ing for a

d) *return to*

their house
and homed

family–famil
iar-terrain.

Lost and found? *(3)*

a) What's be

come of one
of my long–

time most inti

b) mate-readers

She hung–
up–on–me

and remains

c) unreach

able even
through that

poetic–famil
arity.

Me and my *(8)*

a) father Can

one remain

so similar
in appear

b) ance in long-

viewed eye

and mind-
sense in that

absent-mind

c) ed appeal

to one's
most inward

ly-sourced
existen

d) tial-be

ing so-o

therwise-
lifed-with-

antithet
ic-value-

e) claims of

the word

and his
extra-divid

ends My fa

f) ther's-claim-

to–fame
name's inscrib

ed on many
charitable

g) institut

ions whereas

my poems as
DuFu's prepare

h) to wait a

century or

two for ade
quate-recognit

ion.

"Lost and (3)

a) found" what I

remember

of Fox Mea
dow's first–

grade–class

b) What I've

lost remain
s that Scars

dale Jewish
wealth–appeal

What I've

c) found so

much more–
important

faith love
and future

living–hope
s.

Up-to-date *(6)*

a) ness This pre-

morning mid–
February

winter

b) ed darkness

alone with
those over-

sized crow'
s arti

c) culating

some kind of

impending-
danger per

haps for

d) that Putin

called–Ukra
ine while

situated
here more-or–

e) less in poet

ic–isolat

ion with
only the–po

f) wer-of-word

s to recon

cile this up–
to-date

ness.

A still (2)

a) life feeling

perhaps too-

much-on-dis
play can

only become

b) stilled in

the quiet
udes of a

dialogued-
reflective

ness.

Chinesed (3)

a) How can

one Chinese
oneself into

a mental

b) ity so for

eign from
our own and

a pictur
ed–language

c) implying

more than

the eye
can see or

even seem.

Wild wind (3)

a) s of Shel

leyesque–

intention
s bending

b) these lithe-

unleafed–

trees to
the break

ing-point
of torn

c) limbs or

receptive

spring–
time-blossom

ing-appear
ance

s.

She's not (2)

a) the only wo

man I've

met who've
need be tam

ed of their

b) post-traumat

ic masculin
ed-defying

not-so-fully-
launder

ed-past.

Can one (2)

a) take a-work-

of–art com

pletely–on–
its–own–term

s without
biograph

b) ical–remind

ers of why–
it–may–have–

been–birthed–
personal

ly–so.

Can poetry *(3)*

a) be sensed as

the art of

personal
and histori

b) cal trans

formation

s If so
How can we

transform
ourselve

c) s in to-

those–strange

ly–otherwise–
Chinese–per

spective
s.

Crack-pot *(4)*

a) To be call

ed a crack–

pot's indeed
most insult

b) ing whereas

Kleist's

master com
edy deals

with a gen
uine pot

c) cracked as

my personal

experience
while clean

ing-up the
kitchen Who

d) or what be

came of the

crack(ed)-pot
right-down-

the-middle.

A more-or- (2)

a) *less snow*

less–winter

left us un
protected

with the

b) *hard fact*

s of frost
cold and per

sistent
wind–flurr

ies.

Big-bad-wolf (4)

a) ed She awaited

us with a litt
le girl's

demeanor

b) dressed-up

in a little
Red Riding

Hood's mann
er and she

c) a trades-wo

man spoke

in such a
sweetened

way that

d) I began to

feel much
like that

big-bad–
wolf.

Anonymous (4)

a) mass-produced

houses as

those Long
Island veter

b) an one

s after the
war remain

ed so alike
that their

owner and

c) family may

have felt im
personal

ly anony
mously–hous

ed as those

d) North Vietnam

ese soldier
s just dead–

down number
ed–count

s.

Time-reach

when looking-
out also be

comes a look
ing-in to

the darker
and bright

er realms
of one's own

personal
time-reach.

Probing (3)

a) the deep

There's some

thing myster
ious about fish

b) ing those

dark water

s in to the
unseen depth

c) of one's

own (until

then) surfa
cing–appear

ance
s.

That time-

extending
wharf at Ft.

Myer's beach
far-out in

to the wa
ter's self–

determin
ing time–

reach.

Trumpian

He's the
type who im

pulsive
ly jumps

in to sover
eign water

s never-
having-learn

ed–to–swim.

A comfort (2)

a) able umbrell

ared seat

at the water-
side may be

come in time

b) (especially

for the o
ver 80s)

as a-home-
away-from-

home.

Shorties *(3)*

a) Some may con

tinue to appre

ciate most–
of–all these

b) shorties

not only be
cause of

their most
ly–abstract–

character

c) but also be

cause they allow

for one'
s own spacial–

receptiv
ity.

Which way *(4)*

a) ahead After

two years of

watching and
waiting Cor

b) ona's at

first unsus

pected mutat
ions has left

even the so-
called "ex

c) perts" trail

ing behind

as with Spitzweg'
s over-siz

ed-butter
fly-nets

d) with only

their color

ings indicat
ing which-

way-ahead.

Creation (4)

a) al similari

ties Where

Chinese
artistic–

b) poetic-trad

ition at

best meets
our own in

their land

c) scaping es

pecially
birds animal

s and flower

d) ing a myster

ious creat
ional express

ive-fine
ness.

What should (4)

a) one expect

after break
ing with the

tradition

b) al Jewish-A

merican mater
ialism return

ing to the
post–Holo

c) caust Ger

many marrying

a German be
coming a Luth

eran minist

d) er What should

one expect
from one's er

rant-child
ren.

When that (6)

a) really roman

tic image of

the poor-
suffering-

b) artist be

comes pre-con

ditioned for
artistic

and spirit

c) ual freedom

One could
counter that

Affluence
(as with Mendel

d) ssohn) helps

free one from

the-daily-
burden-of-fin

e) ancial-concern

s to an art
istic-spirit

ual-individ
uality

f) We all suffer

rich and poor

from our
own personal-

inconsisten
cies.

Time-telling *(3)*

a) Now that

the storm
has passed a

kind of in
nocent–

b) stillness

pervades

the landscap
ing of this

early morn

c) ing mid-Feb

ruary late
winter's

time-tell
ing.

After being *(4)*

   a) hurt by her

   genuine pre-
   marital choice
   she seems

   b) to have ta

   ken to ex

   changeable
   lovers not

   only as a

   c) means of

   self-satis
   faction

   but perhap

   d) s with more

   than a touch
   of revenge

   ful-instinct
   s.

Can such an (2)

    a) early-morning-

    immovable–

    silence be
    come contag

    ious as a

    b) disease that

    pervades
    the very life–

    pores of one'
    s existen

    tial-being.

Had her (2)

a) very precise

way of order

ing her dress
ed and room

ed-presence

b) been sourced

in those most
inward of

aesthetic
ly self-be

coming-need
s.

He as a (2)

a) successful

tradesman

displaying
a superior

self-orien
ted const

b) ant-presence

bottomed

shirt–wise
with-alter

nating–
button

ed–distinct
ion.

Song of a (3)

a) decaydent

society If

there's no
God no judg

b) ment why be

bound by
more than

c) the earth-

rites-of-
primeval-

instinct
ual-blessing

s.

Fantasy Poem 1 *(4)*

a) If primit

ive cave-hun
ters can

paint the ani
mals they

b) intend to

kill Maybe if

I keep look
ing at that

large gondola-

c) picture of

Venice envis
ioning Bellini

Guardi and
the others

d) they'll take

me right in

to their
very-gondo

la-presen

ce.

A singul

ar rose
attracting

the entire
room with

its most
delicate

ly sensed-
composure.

Fantasy Poem 2 *(2)*

a) Is it real

ly true that
if you paint

ed a Chinese
white falcon

b) so exactly-

imaginative

ly as Dürer
it might

simply fly-
off.

There may (3)

a) remain at

least two

sides to e
very story-

b) situation

But with a

bit of imagin
ation one a

lone could
at least dou

c) ble that Why

then do most

insist on
their own one-

way street-
seeing

s.

Fantasy Poem 3 *(4)*

a) Historical

novels remain
not the only

means of i
magining (our

b) selves) in

other times

and places
Is that an

escape mechan

c) ism from the

present person
time and place

or a post-his

d) torical way

of actually i
magining anoth

er way–
out.

Dark tree

s climbing
the night

air as if
phantomed

from a
blood–swell

ing–curse.

5 am (3)

a) A blank

mind and a
momentary

wordless–re

b) sponse as

if Poem had–
taken–the–

day–off and

c) I still under

the dream–
spell of night'

s darkful–pre
sence.

"Desiring (3)

a) this man's

gift and

that man's
scope" Person

ally I've

b) remained per

haps too
self-satis

fied with
the gifts I'

ve received

c) and the al

most epic
scope of my

widely
themed-ex

pressive
ness.

A common-pre *(2)*

a) sence Corona and

Poem seem
to have acti

vated an
almost comm

b) on-presence

through

their conta
gious long–

lifed appear
ance–sake.

Know-how *(4)*

a) The Corona

rules have

changed so
often per

b) haps imitat

ing its mu

tational-
course while

up–until–

c) now there

seems to re
main no poss

ible means
for catch

d) ing-up with

its e

ver–persua
sive–know–

how.

Of 2nd-rate- (4)

   a) value Has

freedom be

come in the
"home of

the free" a

   b) 2nd-rate-

value constit
utionally

poised again
st dictator

s of most

   c) any-kind

but now per
sonally un

able to list
en–to or e

d) ven tolerate

an equally-

sanction
ed other-

wise point-of-
view.

Why *(4)*

a) have Eastern

Asiatic per

formers
from Japan

China and

b) Korea become

enabled to
personally

interprete
Western classi

cal music

c) while

our own ear
s remain

scarcely-at
tuned to

their strange

d) music and

songfully-
imaged-poet

ic-express
iveness.

Why is it (5)

a) that he from

a tradition

al small-town
Bavarian

b) background

remained so

personal
ly-adventur

ous marrying

c) a Spanish

lady travell
ing profess

ionally
through much–

d) of-the-world

while his

brother re
mained a

perpetual

e) ly-uninter

ested Bavar

ian stay–
at–home.

Unanswer (4)

a) *ed question*

s as with

Charles Ed
ward Ive

b) *s continue*

to stimulate

explora
tive-person

s independ

c) *ent of race*

creed or of

whatever
class per

d) *haps in*

need of a

personal
identity-

cause.

Big car

big roll
big man

Tanked for
more than

self-protect
ive war–game

s on the
German

highway
s.

Nothing fun

ny about
that nervous

laugh so
prevalent

here Better
to remain

speechless
ly self–com

posed.

Fat Cows (2)

a) Some men

and women
here resemble

those bibli
cal fat cow

b) s grazing on

their more-

than-substan
tial sustan

ent home-
bred diet.

Sanctificat (2)

a) ions These heaven

ly-messaging
clouds slowly

transform
ing the blue

of this late

b) winter's

morning in
to a panor

ama of vision
ary-sanctifi

cation
s.

The Japan (3)

a) ese so war-

like Shinto–

Samurai
tradition

b) yet so fine

ly haiku'd
in to but

a touched–
sense poetic

c) tradition

life–styling

much of even
daily–ex

pressive
ness.

Two faced (6)

a) *"America*
first" can
mean either
a George

b) *Washington'*
s inaugurat
ed isolation
ist Manifest
Destiny trad

c) *ition or a*
world power
attempt to
market a
freedom–lov

d) ing American

democrat

ic-tradit
ion Such two-

faced intent

e) ions have

alternate
ly plagued

and/or bless
ed Chinese

f) and Japanese

historical-

ly-orient
ed-respon

se.

Unlimited- *(3)*

a) personal-

expectan
cies My balcon

ied multi-di

b) mensional

gardened-
view has open

ed-out a

c) sense of al

most-unlimit
ed-personal-

expectan
cies.

A cool (2)

a) brightness

as the metall

ic–touch–
of–reflect

ive–expecta

b) tion

s awared
this after

noon's stead
fast–time–ex

posure
s.

Redon'

s mystical
ly–sourced–

sailboat ex
ploring realm

s of darken
ing water'

s previous–
ly unknown

time–expan
ses.

Franz at

age 5 smiled
a rainbow

of childhood-
delight

s.

Adequatedly- *(3)*

a) jewell

ed Some women

must feel ade
quately jewel

b) ly in semi-

precious–

stones reveal
ing even

more than

c) their own

attentive
ly-sourced–

smiling-
length

s.

That pleasur

able feeling
of being em

braced with
affection

ate-time-
holding-ex

pectation
s.

It needn'

t be self-re
solved when

a river
swells bey

ond its
accustom

ed time-at
tending

depth-find
s.

This night

has become
birthed with

an unknown
secret

but silent
ly-withhold

ing-express
iveness.

Alone with (2)

a) myself at

4:30 am

No one
near or far

to be list

b) ening to

these sil
ently self–

invok
ing–messag

ing
s.

What the (2)

a) wind know

s become

s revealed
only through

listening
as hard as

b) one can to

its voice

d ever-pre
sent time-ex

tending here-
and-now.

History (2)

a) recalls what

has actual

ly happen
ed whereas

remembran
ce has be

b) come the

personal

muse in
fear of

what-could-
have-been.

Self-pro (2)

a) tection

seems best

accomplish
ed through

useable
scape-goat

b) s through

the ages
most especial

ly danger
ously-other

wise-Jew
s.

The langu (3)

a) age of dicta

tors (even

minor semi-
establish

b) ed ones as

Putin) re

mains the
best mean

s of con
cealing

c) their own

(perhaps not

yet even
self-reveal

ing) appear
ance

s.

"We shall overcome" (3)

a) Can poetic-

sensibil
ity over

b) come class

race up

bringing
and other

self-deter

c) mining his

torical-
linguist

ic barr
iers.

The-will-to (4)

a) *power Has the*

will-to-power

(biblical
ly pre-deter

b) *mined in*

its snake-
like way)

become the
central cause

c) *of man's con*

tinuous war-

like deviant-
behavior And

has love (sourc
ed-through-

d) Christ's-very-

being) become

the only mean
s of over–

coming that
Satanic-urge.

Concealed message (5)

a) Can the in

comprehen
sible Lord

b)use Satanic

means as pure–

sexual-lust
to overcome

a Satanic

c) power-thir

st Is that
also Shakes

peare's conceal
ed message in

d) his Antony and

Cleopatra

After all His
specially

chosen-one

e) s as David

and Paul
were both (in

their way)
murderer

s.

No future- (4)

a) tellings None-

of–us command

a pre–under
standing

b) of how we'

ll react

under condit
ions of ex

treme–stress

c) as the pre-

Holocaust
German Jews

in the mid
and late 30

s We can

d) only hope and

pray–for–the–
best whatever

that may
mean.

Imaged (4)

a) Step by

step coun

try by coun
try the–Sov

b) iet-success

or Putin's

on his way
of re–estab

lishing most

c) all of what

Russia had
lost He im

pressed in
the image

d) of a czar

or the vic

torious mass–
killer Stal

in.

America (4)

a) the defeat

ed and humil

iated giant
still lick

b) ing its

Vietnam

and Afghan
istan wound

s while

c) stronger

and more o
pen-faced

enemies re

d) placing its

once power-
embellish

ing-post
ure.

It disturb (4)

a) s me that I'

m not the a

vid Christian
I once was

b) propagat

ing the faith

for 3 decade
s that its

flame has

c) cooled as a

candle dried-
down I still

believe – no
question of

that but Poem

d) has replaced

more and more
its own self-

demanding
claim

s.

Identity cause (4)

a) *I'm not e*

ven certain
of my own

raison d'ê

b) *tre still*

very much
our twosome-

oned Am I a
historical

c) *Jew where the*

blood still run

s deep and/or
a Jesus-orient

ed biblical-
Christian

d) *or simply a*

daily two-

hour-poet
and what of

the rest?

Are these (4)

  a) unidenti

  cal twin-

  storms messa
  ging war–

  b) times-ahead

  (and if so

  where's the
  other Ukraine

  or perhaps

  c) that Russian

  Eastern-
  slice) Has

  post–Christ
  ian post-cultur

  al–Europe be

  d) come once a

  gain menaced
  by a self–

  called–dicta
  tor.

True poet (2)

a) s as good

preacher

s are sent
to us to

help quiet-
down to an

b) inward-reflec

tive–resolve

of self–per
petuating

more–last
ing–value

s.

Hand-in-hand (2)

a) First Beijing'

s Olympic

games then
Moscow's war–

time blood–

b) depleting-

games an all
iance of

equally-sour
ced-dictat

ors.

Dangling pre

position
s keep dang

ling their
unfinali

sed ending
s fisher

man's high-
stead.

Circe or (2)

a) Corona As a

power–mind

ed feminist–
young-lady

uncertain

b) whether to

name her
sperm–adopt

ed–daught
er Circe or

Corona.

These wind (2)

a) s remain in

cessant

ly there as
if voiced

without be

b) ginning or

end but never
theless con

stantly
self-deter

mining.

Love as

faith in
need of a

daily renew
al other

wise they
will become

as a boat
timeless

ly abandon
ed.

Reactivated *(2)*

a) In special

times-in-need
as these Cor

ona ones
those pal

b) ed blood-re

lations can be
come once

again fully-
reactiva

ted.

Aging per (3)

a) sons as Rose

marie and

myself favour
a sit-down

b) comfort

ableness

but never
theless re

main uncom

c) fortably attun

ed to these
wind-flee

ing times-
of-our

s.

One might *(3)*

a) feel that

Putin's troops re
situating

the Ukrain

b) ian border re

main fully
prepared for

war's
from-the-

c) onset of their

own blood-

flowing rhy
thmic-de

sign
s.

Those paint (3)

a) *ings (as Ger*

hard Richter

implied) that
create their

b) *own self-sat*

isfying can

vassed–expres
siveness

most certain

c) *ly the one*

s that draw–
me–in to

their very–
presence.

Post-Luther *(3)*

a) an Those who

most alway
s take criti

cism self–

b) defensive

ly as if
disturbing

their own

c) Here I stand

and you're
not going to

tell-me-o
therwise.

Receptiv *(3)*

a) ity of a

most person

al-kind or
of say a

b) work-of-art

may mean the

way I am
and the way

c) I see it

or can-you-

convince-
me-other

wise.

Receptive-aging (6)

a) ness Sitting-

pretty the
way some old-

b) timers most

value their

existenti
ally-aging-

years For o

c) thers aging

may become a
receptive-

denial as my
90-year-old

d) father's

"we're not

old you know"
For still o

thers aging

e) becomes a

time of pre
paredness

While for me

f) aging has be

come a time
of unbeliev

able–creat
ivity.

At certain *(3)*

a) unidentifi

able time

s special
insights pre–

b) determine

the poetic

Word while at
otherwise

times in

c) sights-

through-to-

their-word-
defining

ness.

Fantasy Poem (3)

a) Winter

ing twisted
branches so

imaginary

b) as ghosts and

goblins twis
ting his in

sides–out
into a

long forgot

c) ten fairy

tale time
of child

hood bed–
side imagin

ings.

Sleep-awaken *(3)*

a) ings Softly

felt persuas
ions as a

mother car

b) essing the

cheeks of
her small

child's anxious

c) ly awaiting

bed–side

moon–lit
sleep–awaken

ings.

Appearance- *(3)*

a) sake Previous

ly unnotic
ed buds

awakening

b) a fledgling

tree from
its winter

ed bare-
branched

c) sleep just

nudged for

a momenta
ry appear

ance-sake.

Some per (3)

a) sons remain

so shy so

modest so
reserved

that it

b) takes more

than a litt
le effort

to urge
those most

opportune

c) words from

their hidden
and re

clusive
time–forsak

ening
s.

In the form of a pre (3)

a) lude This late

winter early
morning dark

b) ness has ceased

to become a–

genuine–dialect
ic–partner

The Word it
self must

c) brighten

me through

its time–
telling–ex

posure
s.

February (4)

a) 22 George Wash

ington's birth

day long a
national holi

day but now

b) the leit-fig

ure for a
patriotic

general and
exampling

president

c) yet he as a

Southern
gentleman

possessed
slaves as

d) well Does

that diminish

his central
importance

in American
history.

However (4)

a) much I keep

(re)read

ing Du Fu's
poems however

little I

b) come to real

ise his so
pedestall

ed-greatness
Are the trans

lations re

c) sponsible

and/or my
own subject

ive limitat
ions and/or

does the

d) language

itself barr
ier a full–

acceptan
ce.

Does the loss *(4)*

a) of a friend

become the par

tial loss as well
of our very-

b) self Good

friends help

us realise
a somewhat

special part

c) of our own

identity-
cause

Whereas Rose
marie's death

d) would di

vide my very-

being right–
down-the-

middle.

Tearing- (3)

a) down monument

s of a nat

ional past
not only dis

b) plays a

total lack

of an–histor
ical–sense

but perhaps
indicating

c) a-possible

personal–
future–

suicidal–
attempt.

Why did (5)

a) Juliette

(a woman I

scarcely
knew but

b) daughter

of one of

my parent'
s closest

friends) pre
sent her

c) most-beauti

fying–cancer

ed–self–to–
me perhaps

as a final
parental

d) desparate-

attempt to
annul my

German–bas
ed Christian–

e) marriage

or of a

love con
cealed

to its very–
end.

Beauty (2)

a) has always

remained

the-essen
tial-bait

for fully
hooking our

b) most appre

ciable weak

ness to its
bottom-down (un)

desirable-
end.

Boost (4)

a) ers Did the

boost real
ly booster

one's resis
tance to Cor

b) ona I've

known too

many example
s of an en

tired boosted
laid-low-fam

c) ily by

this virus
Do boost

ed-calls
of pretty

cheer-leaders

d) actually help

or distract
to time-

players in
the field.

When your (3)

a) foot-work

s only un

steadily
that as a

b) young child

you need

call it
back time and

again to re

c) insure a sym

pathetic
ground-bas

ed–certain
ty.

Czar Putin as (4)

a) Trump seem

s to be

misusing
others'

b) genuine Christ

ian prayer

s for his
completely

unchristian

c) personal

power-thirs
ty-goals

They say

d) Those icons

were heard

weeping after
his wordless-

but self-sancti
fying-prayer

s.

Not only do (3)

a) (semi) dictat

ors come in

time to be
lieve their

b) continu

ous lying

but when
they occas

ionally

c) tell-the-

truth they–
must-feel–

totally-un
eased.

Left-out (10)

a) I'm rare

ly informed
of who called

what was said

b) I feel left-

out not be
cause she'

s secret
ive but be

c) cause if she

knows if we'

re really
one that's some

how's enough.

d) Could one

call it self–
protective

the way a
clam clam

s up close

e) s-itself-in-

what's–protect
ively–self–

satisfying?

f) Her beauty'

s of a very
seldom kind

and yet as
she says

g) (but doesn'

t complain)

that boys
never took an

interest in

h) her because

of her relig
ious nature

because of
her very pri

i) vate ways

that increase

s her attract
ion for me

I'm really

j) glad-of-it

but neverthe
less feel at

times a–bit–
left–out.

Are person (3)

a) al things pri

vate shouldn'

t be written a
bout or are

they an inti

b) mate most

self-reveal
ing express

ion of why
Poem demand

s its own

c) right for

those now
or later

who'll take–
a-personal–

interest–too.

Her love (4)

a) and marriage

didn't work-

out that's
perhaps why

b) she's taken-

to-ours not

Rosemarie
or me but

more the-mar

c) riage-it

self as if
such very-pri
vate-truth

d) s-of-other

s could be
come some

how-one's-
own.

Daily read (4)

a) *ing in the*
Bible (Rose
marie's idea)
brought me

b) *back once a*
gain to a
closeness-
in-Christ
Too much
theology –

c) *they were*
Jesus' enemie
s Luther's
as well and
an errant
church distant

d) *me from the*
real source
of my self-
overcoming
faith.

Aging *(4)*

a) aging means

a virtuos
ity of pain

b) s an increase

in doctor's
visits and

a decrease
of physical

c) well-being

It reestab

lishes new
perspect

ives and can

d) open-up new

and essent
ial future–

possibili
ties.

Future prospects *(4)*

a) Crutches

and wheel
chairs are

dominating

b) more and

more transpor
tation's

prospects
even though

I sense

c) Rosemarie

and myself

may become
that way

soon I don'
t turn aside

d) or allow my

self the low

est of most
all feeling

s (self)-pity.

Spoiled *(4)*

a) children

become a

mong those
least able

b) to cope with

life's diffi

cult and var
ied problem

s And I the

c) only son

the youngest
of 3 sibl

ings and
favored my–

life-long

d) fit-in per

fectly well
to that initial

ly-sponsor
ed–category.

Despite (3)

a) these sharp

and cruel

late-winter
ed-winds our

not-over-

b) cultivated-

garden has
answered

not with that
grim and bund

led-up look

c) but has pre

sented us with
a parade of

white and
yellow flow

ering
s.

One (for Rainer) (3)

a) should never

forget as
the–middle

b) ages-Cluny

rediscover
ed that every

poor sick dis
abled person

we meet has

c) become trans

formed from
the merciful

Christ our
Lord.

Is it that (4)

a) *old-German-*

sense-of-super

iority that
enables it

b) *to take a*

high-moral-

stand as
the only

country of

c) *the European*

Community
that refuse

s to send
weapons to

d) *the despar*

ately under

manned-
Ukrain

ians.

There re (6)

a) main two

ways of

writing one'
s autobio

b) graphy (I'

ve written

three-of–
them) either

subjective

c) ly in the

midst of
that self–

telling or
at the more

d) "objective"

end of that

fullness-
lifed Hist

ory remain

e) s faced with

that same
dilemma of

becoming
quickly da

ted or stan

f) ced in a

Rankean so-
called "ob

jective
reality".

That "red- (4)

a) line" Where'

s the Christ

ian border-
line (red-

b) line) between

trying to

understand
one's oppon

ent's point-
of-view–

c) Kiev was so-

to-say Russia'

s first capital
and standing–

up (if necess
arily militar

d) ily) to an un

loveable

dictator's
expansion

ist-desire
s.

Czar Putin (3)

a) the Pan-Slav

ic czar with

his special
brotherly

love for the

b) Ukraine

sliced–it–up
now 3 times

even willing
to divide it

with the

c) brotherly

Poles while
still profess

ing his un–
divided–

love.

One has to *(3)*

a) remain care

ful these

days (despite
so-called

b) freedom-of-

expression)

in the choice
of one's

words As a

c) practicing

poet that's
already be

come our–
daily-fare.

These self- *(3)*

a) abandoning-

clouds moving

ever–so–slow
ly procession

b) ally as those

spatially

conceived
adagios of

Haydn and at

c) times even

of the dramatic
ally-sponsor

ed–Beethov
ian.

Those most (4)

a) critical of

others are

usually
those least

b) capable of

taking self–

criticism
Is their

watch–dog

c) art of criti

cising other
s more-than-

anything-

d) else a mean

s of protect
ing-their-

own–over–sen
sitivity.

Is time *(4)*

a) best measur

ed by blood

y-conquest
s by new

b) and signifi

cant discov

eries by
the wonder

s of enthral

c) ling natural

scenes by
spiritual

art of the
highest qual

ity or simply by

d) the together

ness of a
love-felt

summer-after
noon.

Ukrainians *(2)*

a) as the Kurds

without a

common–nation
al–background

without a
common–faith–

b) without a

common–history

yet somehow a
wared of a

common–des
tiny.

Otherwise *(3)*

a) Two-empty-

handed semi-
disciples

The one left

b) the business

world for my
historical

one The
other one

from my parish

c) discovered

a poet in
stead I con

tinue to move
on in-need-of-

a-new-start.

Franz (3)

a) that little

5-year-old-

boy with the
sunshine

b) smiling his

first two-

wheeled
ride as if

the flower

c) s however

small bloss
oming in

coloring-
accord.

Pure lyri

cal poetry
will alway

s retain its
own special

rights the
very heart

and soul
of the poet

ic-mind.

Listing- (2)

a) poems so comm

on among the

Chinese (or
has it be

come the translator'

b) s fault)

fail in their

spacious
need for

breathing-
sake.

Two top- *(3)*

a) trees-raven

s attend

ant to
their early

b) morning

look-out

posts as
guardian

s of the

c) morning's-

receptive-
suntime-

appear
ance.

"She never (3)

    a) told her love"

(Shakes

peare/Haydn)
Who was it

when and
where secret

    b) ly withhold

ing as a

flower bloom
ed in-speech

less–silen
ces.

Those un (2)

a) said poetic

silence

s as with
Theodor

Storm ex
pressing

b) perhaps e

ven more

than word
s could

possibly
realise.

Appearance- *(3)*

a) sake Keep your

upper-lip
stiff in the

best Brit

b) ish fashion

taking-on
those exact

ing-pain
s as if

c) lessened

to but a

second
ary appear

ance-sake.

If Rosemar (3)

a) *ie's and my*

own identity-

cause have be
come lasting

b) *ly-united*

then perhap

s the heart
and soul of

c) *these poem*

s express

es much of
our rhythm

mic–design
s.

Has this (7)

a) pre-spring

pale blue

sky prescrib
ed a change

b) of heaven

ly-landscap

ing (or other
wise express

ed) is our

c) generation'

s life-ful
filling

claims dy
ing-out be

d) come paled for

a newly es

tablish
ing time-

telling-e
poch

e) That continu

ous–repetit
ive–mirror

ing–image
of no–where

s–me dead–

f) and-absolute

ly–gone leav
ing behind

a world that
had once be

come mine
Goethe's

g) last(ing)

words "more

light" re
flecting a

Christless–
faith?

February 24th (3)

a) When the

alphabet
of war when

blood speak
s its dead

b) ly-urgencie

s how can

the naked
word still be

heard as
man's prevail

c) ing need

for-an-inner-

spiritual-
peace of

mind heart
and soul.

The Ukraine (4)

a) is where the

Germans hous

ed the help
less Jews

b) in to their

bloodless-

charred-re
mains where

Stalin had

c) previous

ly hunger
ed million

s to death'
s untimely-hold

Ukraine now

d) Putin's

carefully
orchestrat

ed grave
yard.

Putin (4)

a) He chose

the ideal mo
ment when

America was

b) still lick

ing Afgh
anistan'

s humiliat
ing-wounds

when Germany

c) on its moral

high-horse
refused to

deliver the
most necess

ary weapon

d) s He articu

latedly timed
his death-in

voking-mess
age.

Games (3)

a) First the

Olympic

games then
the games–

b) of-war Has

man discover

ed no better
means of ex

hibiting
his muscul

ar agility

c) than those

once so play

ful Breughel
ian–child

hold–game
s.

Has Putin (3)

a) short-term

ed over-

stepped-his-
mark If

b) free Europe

unites not

only militar
ily to de

fend even
with increas

c) ing force

its freedom-

aspiring-de
mocratic-

way-of-
life.

Is it only (3)

a) in times of

war that we

begin to
fully appre

b) ciate the-

blessings–

–of–peace
Tolstoy's

great master

c) piece documen

ted that in–
the–most–con

vincing–man
ner.

Life it (5)

a) self has be

come endanger

ed now on
many front

b) s war plague

and (un)nat

ural occurren
ces of numer

ous kinds

c) Man himself

has remain

ed mostly
responsi

ble for many

d) of these

My (un)allow
ed question

for the
Good Lord

If you

e) needed

(wanted)
a partner

why did
you choose

us.

In Nomine
Domini!
February 24
2022

P. S. (5)

   a) "his eyes

   were bigger
   than his

   stomach" Putin

   b) had earlier

   carefully
   prepared for

   his final 3–
   part-takeover

   c) slicing off

   Ukraine's

   landscap
   ing bit by

   bit This Time

d) (surprising

us all) he
went for the

whole which

e) will remain

in many re
spects too

big to swall
ow-down.

Poetry books by David Jaffin

1. **Conformed to Stone,** Abelard-Schuman, New York 1968, London 1970.

2. **Emptied Spaces,** with an illustration by Jacques Lipschitz, Abelard-Schuman, London 1972.

3. **In the Glass of Winter,** Abelard-Schuman, London 1975, with an illustration by Mordechai Ardon.

4. **As One,** The Elizabeth Press, New Rochelle, N. Y. 1975.

5. **The Half of a Circle,** The Elizabeth Press, New Rochelle, N. Y. 1977.

6. **Space of,** The Elizabeth Press, New Rochelle, N. Y. 1978.

7. **Preceptions,** The Elizabeth Press, New Rochelle, N. Y. 1979.

8. **For the Finger's Want of Sound,** Shearsman Plymouth, England 1982.

9. **The Density for Color,** Shearsman Plymouth, England 1982.

10. **Selected Poems** with an illustration by Mordechai Ardon, English/Hebrew, Massada Publishers, Givatyim, Israel 1982.

11. **The Telling of Time,** Shearsman Books, Kentisbeare, England 2000 and Johannis, Lahr, Germany.

12. **That Sense for Meaning,** Shearsman Books, Kentisbeare, England 2001 and Johannis, Lahr, Germany.

13. **Into the timeless Deep,** Shearsman Books, Kentisbeare, England 2003 and Johannis, Lahr, Germany.

14. **A Birth in Seeing,** Shearsman Books, Exeter, England 2003 and Johannis, Lahr, Germany.

15. **Through Lost Silences,** Shearsman Books, Exeter, England 2003 and Johannis, Lahr, Germany.

16. **A voiced Awakening,** Shearsman Books, Exter, England 2004 and Johannis, Lahr, Germany.

17. **These Time-Shifting Thoughts**, Shearsman Books, Exeter, England 2005 and Johannis, Lahr, Germany.

18. **Intimacies of Sound,** Shearsman Books, Exeter, England 2005 and Johannis, Lahr, Germany.

19. **Dream Flow** with an illustration by Charles Seliger, Shearsman Books, Exeter, England 2006 and Johannis, Lahr, Germany.

20. **Sunstreams** with an illustration by Charles Seliger, Shearsman Books, Exeter, England 2007 and Johannis, Lahr, Germany.

21. **Thought Colors,** with an illustration by Charles Seliger, Shearsman Books, Exeter, England 2008 and Johannis, Lahr, Germany.

22. **Eye-Sensing,** Ahadada, Tokyo, Japan and Toronto, Canada 2008.

23. **Wind-phrasings,** with an illustration by Charles Seliger, Shearsman Books, Exeter, England 2009 and Johannis, Lahr, Germany.

24. **Time shadows,** with an illustration by Charles Seliger, Shearsman Books, Exeter, England 2009 and Johannis, Lahr, Germany.

25. **A World mapped-out,** with an illustration by Charles Seliger, Shearsman Books, Exeter, England 2010.

26. **Light Paths,** with an illustration by Charles Seliger, Shearsman Books, Exeter, England 2011 and Edition Wortschatz, Schwarzenfeld, Germany.

27. **Always Now,** with an illustration by Charles Seliger, Shearsman Books, Bristol, England 2012 and Edition Wortschatz, Schwarzenfeld, Germany.

28. **Labyrinthed,** with an illustration by Charles Seliger, Shearsman Books, Bristol, England 2012 and Edition Wortschatz, Schwarzenfeld, Germany.

29. **The Other Side of Self,** with an illustration by Charles Seliger, Shearsman Books, Bristol, England 2012 and Edition Wortschatz, Schwarzenfeld, Germany.

30. **Light Sources,** with an illustration by Charles Seliger, Shearsman Books, Bristol, England 2013 and Edition Wortschatz, Schwarzenfeld, Germany.

31. **Landing Rights,** with an illustration by Charles Seliger, Shearsman Books, Bristol, England 2014 and Edition Wortschatz, Schwarzenfeld, Germany.

32. **Listening to Silence,** with an illustration by Charles Seliger, Shearsman Books, Bristol, England 2014 and Edition Wortschatz, Schwarzenfeld, Germany.

33. **Taking Leave,** with an illustration by Mei Fêng, Shearsman Books, Bristol, England 2014 and Edition Wortschatz, Schwarzenfeld, Germany.

34. **Jewel Sensed,** with an illustration by Paul Klee, Shearsman Books, Bristol, England 2015 and Edition Wortschatz, Schwarzenfeld, Germany.

35. **Shadowing Images**, with an illustration by Pieter de Hooch, Shearsman Books, Bristol, England 2015 and Edition Wortschatz, Schwarzenfeld.

36. **Untouched Silences**, with an illustration by Paul Seehaus, Shearsman Books, Bristol, England 2016 and Edition Wortschatz, Schwarzenfeld.

37. **Soundlesss Impressions**, with an illustration by Qi Baishi, Shearsman Books, Bristol, England 2016 and Edition Wortschatz, Schwarzenfeld.

38. **Moon Flowers**, with a photograph by Hannelore Bäumler, Shearsman Books, Bristol, England 2017 and Edition Wortschatz, Schwarzenfeld.

39. **The Healing of a Broken World**, with a photograph by Hannelore Bäumler, Shearsman Books, Bristol, England 2018 and Edition Wortschatz, Cuxhaven.

40. **Opus 40**, with a photograph by Hannelore Bäumler, Shearsman Books, Bristol, England 2018 and Edition Wortschatz, Cuxhaven.

41. **Identity Cause**, with a photograph by Hannelore Bäumler, Shearsman Books, Bristol, England 2018 and Edition Wortschatz, Cuxhaven.

42. **Kaleidoscope**, with a photograph by Hannelore Bäumler, Shearsman Books, Bristol, England 2019 and Edition Wortschatz, Cuxhaven.

43. **Snow-touched Imaginings**, with a photograph by Hannelore Bäumler, Shearsman Books, Bristol, England 2019 and Edition Wortschatz, Cuxhaven.

44. **Two-timed**, with a photograph by Hannelore Bäumler, Shearsman Books, Bristol, England 2020 and Edition Wortschatz, Cuxhaven.

45. **Corona Poems**, with a photograph by Hannelore Bäumler, Shearsman Books, Bristol, England 2020 and Edition Wortschatz, Cuxhaven.

46. **Spring Shadowings**, with a photograph by Hannelore Bäumler, Shearsman Books, Bristol, England 2021 and Edition Wortschatz, Cuxhaven.

47. **October: Cyprus Poems**, with an illustration by Odilon Redon, Shearsman Books, Bristol, England 2021 and Edition Wortschatz, Cuxhaven.

48. **Snow Dreams**, with a photograph by Hannelore Bäumler, Shearsman Books, Bristol, England 2022 and Edition Wortschatz, Cuxhaven.

Book on David Jaffin's poetry: Warren Fulton, **Poemed on a beach,** Ahadada, Tokyo, Japan and Toronto, Canada 2010.